Dedicated to
My Mom and Dad Who Made It
All Possible

# INTRODUCTION

In September, 1976, I received the first individual grant from the Nevada State Council on the Arts and set aside time to photograph the decaying wood and abandoned ruins of Nevada. The entire project became an experience.

Life is a constant inward revelation. I have found photoaphy to be a visual expression for this thrilling experience.

Ever since my first trip to Virginia City, I remained fascinated by the standing structures left from the early pioneers. There was a history I felt worth revealing. I went out to tell a story in pictures of man's use of wood and decided to limit my story to this material; for it presented an intriguing scene to my eye. I felt as if I were a lucky individual with a rare glance at what might soon be no longer available for anyone else to see. I felt I had only one opportunity to see this rapidly vanishing scene and 'poof' it would be gone.

Nevada is mostly public land and many of the ruins are unprotected from the bitter climate and brutal vandalism. Many scenes I returned to for a second look were no longer in existence and I felt honored that my camera was able to obtain the Last Look.

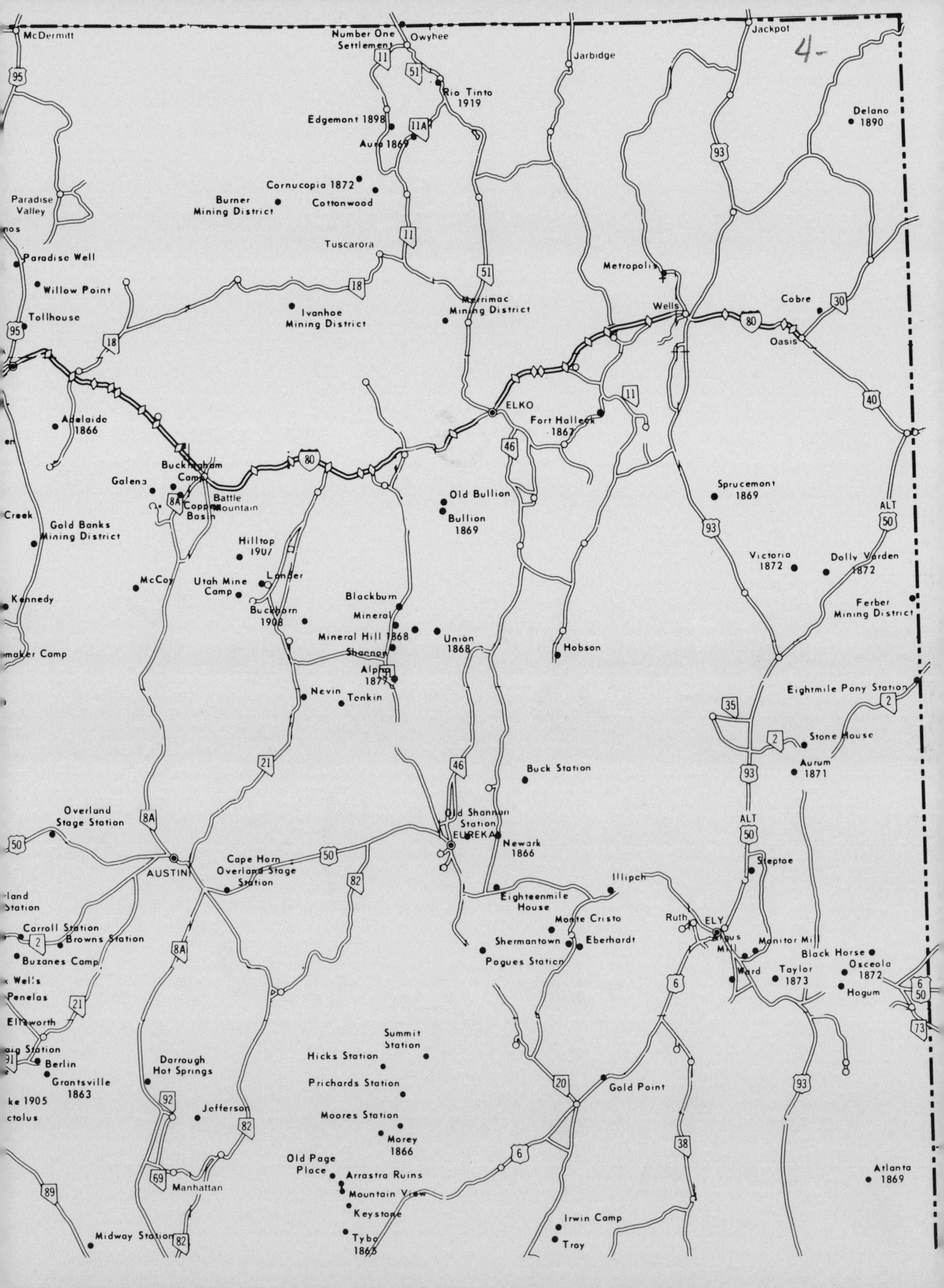

# A LAST LOOK

*Best Wishes!*

*[signature]*

# ACKNOWLEDGMENTS

I would like to acknowledge all the many people who poured their soul into making this book a reality. My first thanks goes to the Nevada State Council on the Arts who had the courage to grant me their first monies to an individual. For their trust and encouragement. I would also like to thank the many people I met in Nevada's ghost towns who helped me find my way around to the ruins and offered assistance and their personal recollections of the past. I would also like to thank the following people for the input and help in editing, criticism and encouragement. They are not given in order of importance, for they were all important. Bruce Lindsay, Loree Sutton, David Cavignarro, Ansel Adams, John Andrews, Donna Leonard, Tony Evans, Spencer Hobson and John Jepson, Mike Yordy, Ethel Pittman, Howard Hickson, and Sue Mersing and Marty Rehm, of Diamond Typeset, for their help in editing, layout, and book design.

# *A LAST LOOK*

Photography
by
*Louis F. DeSerio*

Text
by
*Glen H. Greenwell, Jr.*

Published
by
*Louis F. DeSerio*

©Copyright 1979, Louis F. DeSerio and Glen H. Greenwell, Jr.

All rights reserved in all countries.
No part of this book may be reproduced
or translated in any form, including
microfilming, without permission in
writing from the authors and publishers.

Louis F. DeSerio, Publisher
Post Office Box 22
Beckwourth, California 96129

International Standard Book No. 0-9603568-0-0

Library of Congress Catalog Card No. 79-67536

Printed in the U.S.A.

This first edition of *The Last Look,* designed
by Louis F. DeSerio, was printed in October, 1979.
Typography is Souvenir and Kaylin, set by
Diamond Typeset, Reno. Offset lithography is
by Cardinal Printing Company, San Francisco.
Reproductions are printed in 200 line screen with
the alpha tint process on Warren's 100# Cameo Dull
book. Text paper is Simpson's 80# Teton Ivory.

*After traveling and photographing the state for two years, a story began to emerge in the very core of my soul. A story that unfolds much like a piece of music, with a theme, a melody and rhythm. The visual world is now heard and its melody sings with words.*

*What you are about to experience is two voices singing a song in harmony, playing the same melody, keeping the same beat and we invite you to tap along and feel the rhythm. The song is as old as man and as long as men walk the earth, a song we need never forget.*

*When I encountered the following tale written by Glen, although it does not deal with Nevada per se, I felt that he captured in words the mood which I strove to capture in my photography.*

*Louis F. DeSerio*
Beckwourth, California

*It was somewhere in the deserts, covered with the crumbling, rubbled ruins of a once greater glory, where I was sitting, staring at those huge monoliths, fingers pointing to infinity. I was wondering about who or what had created this, for what now vain purpose, to what greater glory and how it must have been to have seen it in its greatness and splendor. I, an observer of another time, was passing by to decipher any message these silent heaps might convey — death, decaying slowly, atom by atom, being ground into the dust of the desert. What truths this once great bastion revealed, whatever message its strength protected, or proclaimed, lay long quieted in the sand, silenced by a restless, prevailing wind, grinding dust into dust, ceaselessly shifting the sand into endlessly wandering forms, constantly changing the terrain, sweeping and molding its features into profiles, shaping each dune into its alter ego, then into nothingness, forcing each one to surrender its identity, capturing each grain of sand and carrying it to yet another eternal destination, replanting each grain, ever-duringly sculpturing infinite variations into an endless rehersal of monotonously familiar forms, blowing the sand, but never blowing it away.*

*I became aware of a man sitting directly in front of me. His skin and eyes were dark and his body was covered with what I considered to be an overburden of clothes which could only add to the already stifling and unbearable heat. But I could see in his smooth, unlined face that he was quite at ease and that he had acquired the wisdom of being patient with the desert. He was staring at me but not a stare that threatened, but more as if he were seeing into me to discover something that he could understand. We said nothing: I because I could not speak his tongue and he, it seemed, because he felt the need for silence. His face was neither young nor old but his eyes seemed to perceive with such insight that their dark depths revealed of having seen a timeless wisdom which, at least until now, had always escaped me. He reached his hands out in a gesture of friendship and I took them into mine and we sat there, silent, like the desert being crevassed by the wind.*

*"Why here?" he asked.*

*I looked at him not knowing what to say.*

*"But that is your question," he continued. "You ask why these ruins are here and since you do not know, you pass your own judgment on what you see before you and in your frame of reference, with whatever knowledge you have, you feel that you are qualified and competent to pass this judgment and perhaps you are, but before I begin I only wish to tell you that there are many sides to reality and we can find the greatest truths in the humblest of things, even here in this desolate, decaying place. You see this only as a place once strong and great and proud and that it, in time, along with all that it was, passed away, perished into the*

*dust and is now forever silent. Here, you think, death stands triumphant and you cite the stillness and decay as being in support of your judgment. What you say is true but even truth is relative.*

*"Everything has its beginning beyond the beginning so where do we begin? In the cosmos where the matter of all that is was once scattered, finding that the stuff from which we have been created is eternal, merely altered into different forms? We must travel through time, to an existence now altered beyond our ability to recognize so that we may come to know what this is. Existence is like this desert, being constantly reshapen into an endless pattern of dunes, ever none exactly the same, each pattern fading away and emerging into another, each the genesis and continuation of yet another and so it is that we too must come to recognize reality in its many different forms and be able to recognize that each separate part is never a final statement but merely a continuation of things, a state of constant becoming and if we can seize on the appearance of what **is**, we can expand it into a continuum of past, present and future and so it is here. What we see now is but the microcosm of a universal truth, the ever universal altering of reality or should we say, the ever altering reality of the universe, an infinite variety of form? If we care to look closely, reality is never disguised beyond recognition but only beyond the comprehension of our ignorance. It is more often that we fail to look closely enough, to search far enough, to perceive with enough*

*clarity to recognize the truth. It is not so much a matter of not being incapable, but of casting ourselves into a convenient mold which requires little but that we survive and do it as comfortably as possible and this most often does not bring us to a higher level of awareness. In our own cycle of life it is important to be conscious of this and to recognize the many multi-formed veils which separate us from this awareness as they so separate one reality from another and if we can only begin to remove them and see beyond, we will see emerging a universal pattern of sameness that unites all things. It is only our **ignorance** which makes distinctions; it is our **wisdom** which gives unity and completeness to reality. Our ignorance makes distinctions because we cannot see with our intellect the wholeness of reality, so we glance at a reflection of its many separate entities like looking at the separate pieces of a puzzle, but so intent at studying the pieces that we fail to put the puzzle together and unite the separate aspects of reality into a complete whole. If we are to have a proper understanding of the things that confront us, let us take the example before us, these scattered ruins and give them unity and perceive this with the wisdom of a different age and with the eyes of a different reality. So for the sake of doing this, let us go through time, even though one second is the same as the next, into ancient antiquity, but when or where it is on the spiral of infinity, I do not know. I only know that it is, somewhere in the continuum of eternity and things,* *neither past nor future, for even they are only an ever merging synthesis of the present.*

*"If we give to these ruins the shape of a structural identity as man once chose to define and build it, we can see the deliberation of his intellect and his planning, how each stone took its place on yet another to give shape and definition to reality as he thought it should be, another monument in the clockwork of time, another monument pointing to eternity. We build them still, simply that **we** might endure, to give permanence to our existence long after we are gone. And so it is that in each generation, yet another monument is raised, leaving yet another legacy for someone else to see, striving to capture in these monuments a moment in time and arrest it for all eternity.*

*"What have we here? Arches and columns in various forms of disarray, unsymetrically juxtaposed, a contradiction to the orderliness and unity it once contained and it is for us to unscramble this confusing paradox to give identity and unity to that reality which we cannot sometimes recognize. Once this was a great moment. The walls, ever crumbling, can still be seen and what was once a bustling community, now lies shattered upon these grounds. Even in its ruin this is, as you can see, still most impressive. And what is it? A temple raised to the glory of God, a gift from a man who claimed that God had bestowed upon him a perfect love, a woman of rare beauty and grace, dark and*

*mysterious like the night, a profound mystery, but a mystery that enchants and entices, a mystery that takes your senses beyond this reality, transforms, transfigures you, giving ecstasy and peace. This is a shrine to that woman, to that love he shared with her, his knowing her, smelling her rich fragrance, feeling the wanton passion of her kiss, the lush ripeness of her body, the subtle beauty reflected in her dark and shining hair. And to this, the ultimate experience, the ultimate expression of his humanity, to know love, to feel a woman's knowing touch, to feel her perfect grace, to have the essence of life united into him, becoming and being one, it is to this he built. Some say his name has been forgotten and others say that legend gives to this anonymous builder the name of Laman. The more he came to love her, the more magnificant his shrine became. There were nights of ecstasy and days of immortality, of having experienced something that will never die, of bliss and beauty that we, alone and apart from woman, can never know, the immortality of love. He loved her so deeply, so intensely, that he so desired that if there was any aspect of his existence upon which he could bestow the gift of immortality, it would be to the awareness of loving her, knowing the bliss, the beauty, grace and enrapturement of her presence before and within him, bestowing upon him the beatitudes of life, of his love taking him into her, with each touch, each kiss and embrace taking them to a new and ever transcending reality, transcending on the ecstasy of infinite, perfect pleasure. This is what he possessed, the feel, the touch of unadorned and naked flesh, of bodies entwined in the rhythmic, undulating embrace of life, opulent with beauty, flowing with a tideless time, feeling, knowing the presence of perfect oneness; immortality,* ***immersed in immortality,*** *till he was no longer man and she no longer woman, but God and Goddess united in the absolute.*

*"What can be said of such love? To the honor and perpetuation, to the immortality of this he built and for all of eternity this was to be his legacy, his captured moment in time. You need only look around and you can still see the faded, fractured image of a once great beauty, a magnificance that time can never destroy, here in these very structures withering away in the dust. Could you or I have accomplished so much in even ten lifetimes and do we possess a capacity for such love?*

*"Laman continued to build; the monument, being never finished, growing in proportion to his love, ever greater, ever higher until it became a mountain upon these plains, its symmetry and beauty came to be known as the wonder of any universe and it was this moment, this love he captured in immortality for all of time.*

*"And then one day it happened. The mountains began to tremble, tumble and crumble into the plains, like sand being poured from a child's playful hands. The world shook with the*

*violence of which the echo alone would have sufficed to destroy all that it touched, cracking the whole earth like you and I would crack an egg. Laman's shrine was destroyed and by some miracle he emerged from that, from these silenced ruins where we now sit. And for Laman, death would have been far better than the cursed blessing of life. His temple, his shrine, his monument lay shattered in the dust and beneath its fell rubble, the woman he loved, dead. He turned his face to the heavens, his eyes blinded by tears of grief and then he screamed out in utter abject agony, 'My God, why has Thou forsaken me?' and with that he turned his face into the hot and forbidding desert, and journied through time, each and every step taking him farther from the beginnings of his existence, as he knew and walked his hell, ever inevitably closer to ultimate nothingness and here in this vast desert, alone and lonely, forsaken and utterly lost, surrounded by the quiet ugliness of death, he died.*

"*With his death remains a continuity. This is our eternal process (that all things remain, but they never remain the same) interweaving through our flesh and sinew. We watch this procession through the ages. The awareness of it begins with the unfolding of life through our first breath, is then magnified with love deeply sighed and is lamented with life forever gone. We know sadness with the passing away of things, with the watching of bits and pieces falling away from our lives, with the erasing of things we know, which once had place and purpose and now await to be forgotten, yet deserve to be remembered.*

*"Here, in the desolation of these ruins, we share Laman's fragile world of love and tragedy. We take our turn, we make our brief passage, and we too drift like sand in the desert which carries us beyond death and unto re-creation, only to **become** something else.*

# *A LAST LOOK*

*Distracted by all the meaningless events in our lives, our minds become cluttered and make it difficult to listen to the quiet. And yet this is the sound we should hear.*

*In the quiet of Nevada's desert, one realizes how little you need and in that process one becomes aware that Cadillacs are not necessary. Simplicity releases the spirit.*

New Horizons

are

before us.

Open and wide

as far as the eye can see,

a land where the only barriers are

those rivers,

streams

and

mountains

which

sustain our existence.

Upon the mountains,
into
the wilderness
man came

*To*

*Seek*

*His*

*Fortune*

# To Build,

# To Live,

# To Love,

## And man's presence is ever felt.

*Where he chose to remain, Man marked that well, fashioning for himself a creative way of life that is unique unto him.*

Even in the remote wilderness

he sought

to adorn

things he made

and

in

his own modest way, showed

that he possessed a certain recognition

of

the ideal

There is always a time when we want to be

intimately aware,

a time to see our reflection,

a time to pass judgment,

a time to be comfortable with happy approval

a time to reflect with sorrow.

*I have found in both my personal life and in other people's lives, there are times when we feel a strong attraction for the darkness. It seems as if there are moments when I want to be depressed, when I want to photograph something that causes pain. When I feel the necessity to cry.*

*It is an important moment for then is when I stop and take inventory of myself and my surroundings. In this reflection I remove pieces that do not fit my puzzle and in this process discover pieces that complete the picture, the thought, the reason and cause for existence.*

*His destiny*
*would*
*often*
*take him elsewhere*

*In his mind*
*He conceived beauty and with his will*
*and*
*hands he brought it to reality.*

*Yet beauty has often to be sacrificed  
for the practical  
and  
suddenly  
we are in a different world, where  
the practical distracts us from the ideal.*

Harsh and demanding
where
the only comfort is of the mind.

But there is an eternal cry
that
reminds one of the deepest moment
when one is alone with mind and spirit.

Progress is best only when it is orderly

and

we can look on those things which made that progress possible

with

dignity and respect.

In many ways the home and the wagon have measured the progress

of man

and

with the coming of both to this land

the burdens and cares

of life

became lighter. Life was made easier and more enjoyable.

His tools become stronger,
His forms of power ever larger —
Power is essential to his ambitions for conquest.
There is a hush before the storm —
it portends the coming of something very powerful,
a realization of majesty
that comes with complete mastery as
man suddenly realizes
he has the ability to create unlimited power.
There was a will, a determination to dig into the
earth,
revealing both his strength
and
his weakness.

*The relationship required to build those structures out of nothing, in the middle of the desert required an effort and a will to achieve and succeed despite the obstacles. A relationship where discipline and perseverance were necessary qualities to survive. It was an important time for man who quests for freedom. But man never seems to attain freedom as long as he keeps searching for gold.*
*And yet as I look around me, I see the frantic quest for gold still alive in people's hearts. Lives are directed for the elusive myth,*
*of gold, the source of happiness.*

And these silent symbols have fallen prey to a vandalizing nature, in man and the toll of time, wasting these fragile remnants of the past. Yet, they are a reminder of life once breathed, once lived, once felt. From these ruins, another line, another page is added to the history of man.

Now only the mute monuments remain, scattered,
skeletal and splintered,
giving testimony to the excitement and enthusiasm
now dead.

The old makes way for the new. Today is used to measure yesterday, for that is man's inheritance. The search for gold and the quest for truth are perennial companions and bringing them to a common ground are old wagons splintered by time. The wagon offered these dreams mobility, but something offered these pursuits refuge and permanence. Old wooden houses, now embraced by nature claiming back to the earth that which man had cut and torn away.

*Why, you may ask, the attraction for scenes of wood? As I travelled through Nevada, I felt an attraction for ruins and abandoned structures grow within me. The wood began to speak. It spoke clearly of days gone by and lamented in its loneliness. Now, left unattended, it decays and collapses.*

*It has not been my intention to glamorize the West or sensationalize Nevada Wood.*

*But rather, it has been to reveal the beauty that lies behind the veil of decay.*

*There is a mystery, and yet there is a meaning to these remaining remnants.*

*Nevada is, perhaps, one of the few places on earth where a man can be out in the silence of eternity. In this silence, one hears.*

*The wood stands as a monument to peace.*

*Louis F. DeSerio*

*Glen H. Greenwell, Jr.*

*Biographies* • *Table of Photographs*

# Glen H. Greenwell, Jr.

*Glen was born on August 21, 1938 in Onalska, Washington. When he was about two, the family settled in Lakeside, Utah, on the western shores of the Great Salt Lake. This provided an early desert experience for Glen. That experience enabled the young child to know peace and possess silence as his friend.*

*He started writing poems and short stories in grade school. Later, while in high school in Wells, Nevada, he wrote articles for the school paper and journalism. He was graduated from high school in 1957. Glen then spent three years in the Army and was stationed in Germany. Back in the States, he was graduated from the University of Nevada in 1967 after majoring in foreign languages. After '67 he went into business management. In 1975, Glen met art photographer Louis DeSerio and from this meeting has grown a lasting friendship. Lou's love for the desert, its sense of beauty and peace, its essence captured in photography, revealed a common love for that which is simple, peaceful and quiet. The relationship of this friendship is a natural blend for their two arts.*

*To Glen, peace is man's number-one priority. "We are scared with devastation and the path to peace is distrustful." It is one of the purposes in Glen's writing to instill the awareness of peace as being essential to the evolution of man. When at peace, man can create.*

## Louis F. DeSerio

*Born in New York City on February 1, 1951, Lou was raised and received his primary education in New York City. Lou attended State University of New York and Brooks Institute of Photography, Santa Barbara, California, studying both music and photography.*

*At the age of three, Lou started playing the piano seriously, with formal lessons not starting until age six when they could find a teacher who would take such a young child. At age 15 he became a professional musician, forming his own band and also playing in other bands. He began teaching at the New York Institute of Music at the age of 17. He has since been a Studio Musician for Columbia Records, New York City, a solo pianist and a pianist with bands. He actively plays the piano and is a composer of music.*

*With the background discipline of music, at age 15, Lou turned to photography to further express his personal growth. While attending State University of New York, he felt that his personal expression in both music and art photography were being smothered by the classroom structure. To fulfill a lifelong fascination of the West, he left New York and hitch-hiked to California. Finding jobs as stock clerk, mailman, house painter, service station attendant, microfilm trainee, and waiter in summer resorts to further pursue his career in photography and music, he once again returned to the classroom. Again feeling smothered, he left the classroom to "experience while learning" rather than "learning without experiencing."*

*Lou much prefers Art Photography to Commercial Photography although most of the time since 1973 has been spent doing commercial photography. He has exhibited, both publicly and privately, extensively in California and Nevada with limited exhibits in New York City. Lou was co-founder of Reno's Photographer's Co-Op, this being the first of its kind in the Reno Area. He has taken numerous private workshops and is currently teaching Photography Workshops. In 1977 he received a grant from the Nevada State Council on the Arts to study with Ansel Adams.*

*Being heavily inspired by Ansel Adams, who is also musician-turned-photographer, Lou feels "photography is a coordination of art with a natural carry-over of music." When operating a camera he is "literally playing the camera, doing a solo, every picture being a composition with elements of rhythm, harmony, balance, coordinated structure of form, with lighting the main melody — or better said, lighting is the 'key'." Sometimes when he's really into playing music, he has visual experiences. And sometimes, when he's totally involved in photography, it's like hearing music. Thus to him, the subject of a photograph can form a visual symphony.*

*"An artist can stay in his living room all his life painting, a photographer has to deal with the real world and penetrate it so he can get a picture, otherwise the picture remains a shadow image."*

*To Louis DeSerio, life is a constant balance between teaching and doing . . . . "Doing gives me something to teach. I'll probably live life out this way."*

## TABLE OF PHOTOGRAPHS

Page

|   | |
|---|---|
|   | Frontispiece: Porch, Goldfield, Nevada 1976 |
| 1 | Old Cabin, Lake Tahoe, Nevada 1977 |
| 2 | Door Knob, Wellington, Nevada 1976 |
| 3 | Windmill, Seven Troughs, Nevada 1977 |
| 6 | Stump in Washoe Valley, Reno, Nevada 1977 |
| 8 | Saw Handle, Beatty, Nevada 1976 |
| 9 | Warped Lumber, Manhattan, Nevada 1976 |
| 10 | Old Door, Goldfield, Nevada 1976 |
| 11 | Hand Saw, Reno, Nevada 1977 |
| 12 | Tools, Ferretto Ranch, Reno, Nevada 1977 |
| 13 | Homestead, Manhattan, Nevada 1976 |
| 14 | Old Couple, Pyramid Lake, Nevada 1977 |
| 15 | Pots and Pans, Goldfield, Nevada 1976 |
| 16 | High Chair, Tuscarora, Nevada 1977 |
| 17 | Jug on Wall, Virginia City, Nevada 1978 |
| 18 | Souvenirs, Midas, Nevada 1976 |
| 19 | Gingerbread, Manhatten, Nevada 1976 |
| 20 | Carved Pheasants, Virginia City, Nevada 1977 |
| 21 | Front Door of The Castle, Virginia City, Nevada 1977 |
| 22 | The Castle, Virginia City, Nevada 1977 |
| 24 | St. Mary's Interior, Virginia City, Nevada 1978 |
| 26 | Pictures on Wall, Eureka, Nevada 1977 |
| 27 | Old Dresser, Reno, Nevada 1977 |
| 28 | Wall Hangings, Virginia City, Nevada 1976 |
| 29 | Burnt Dresser, Tonopah, Nevada 1976 |
| 30 | Burnt Vanity, Tonopah, Nevada 1976 |
| 31 | Peeled Paint, Mina, Nevada 1977 |

| | |
|---|---|
| 32 | Broken Wagon Wheel, Reno, Nevada 1978 |
| 33 | Wagon Hub, Olinghouse, Nevada 1977 |
| 34 | Wagon Hitch, Ferretto Ranch, Reno, Nevada 1977 |
| 35 | Old Buckboard, Reno, Nevada 1977 |
| 36 | Model A Pick-up, Truck, Reno, Nevada 1977 |
| 37 | Snow Storm, Olinghouse, Nevada 1977 |
| 38 | Abandoned Wagon, Olinghouse, Nevada 1977 |
| 39 | Wooden Plow, Reno, Nevada 1978 |
| 40 | Virginia and Truckee Boxcar, Sparks, Nevada 1977 |
| 41 | Broken Wheel, Olinghouse, Nevada 1977 |
| 42 | Cemetery, Eureka, Nevada 1977 |
| 43 | Hand Tools, Olinghouse, Nevada 1977 |
| 44 | Old Chair, Gerlach, Nevada 1977 |
| 45 | Commode, Berlin, Nevada 1977 |
| 46 | Bottle and Hoe, Unionville, Nevada 1977 |
| 47 | Women, Panaca, Nevada 1977 |
| 48 | Washtub and Board, Virginia City, Nevada 1977 |
| 50 | House Frame, Rawhide, Nevada 1977 |
| 52 | Ruins, Rochester, Nevada 1977 |
| 54 | Standing Mill, Olinghouse, Nevada 1977 |
| 55 | Head Frame and Powerline, Fitting, Nevada 1977 |
| 56 | Tracks, Rochester, Nevada 1977 |
| 57 | Mine and Shacks, Midas, Nevada 1977 |
| 58 | Head Frame, Goldfield, Nevada 1977 |
| 60 | Crumbling Mill, Paradise Valley, Nevada 1976 |
| 61 | Broken Ladder, Atlas Mine 1977 |
| 62 | Roof Shingles, Silver City, Nevada 1976 |
| 64 | Old Warehouse, Ione, Nevada 1977 |
| 65 | Collapsed House, Goldfield, Nevada 1976 |
| 66 | Stamp Mill, Pine Grove, Nevada 1977 |
| 68 | Window in Hallway, Winters Ranch, Washoe City, Nevada 1977 |

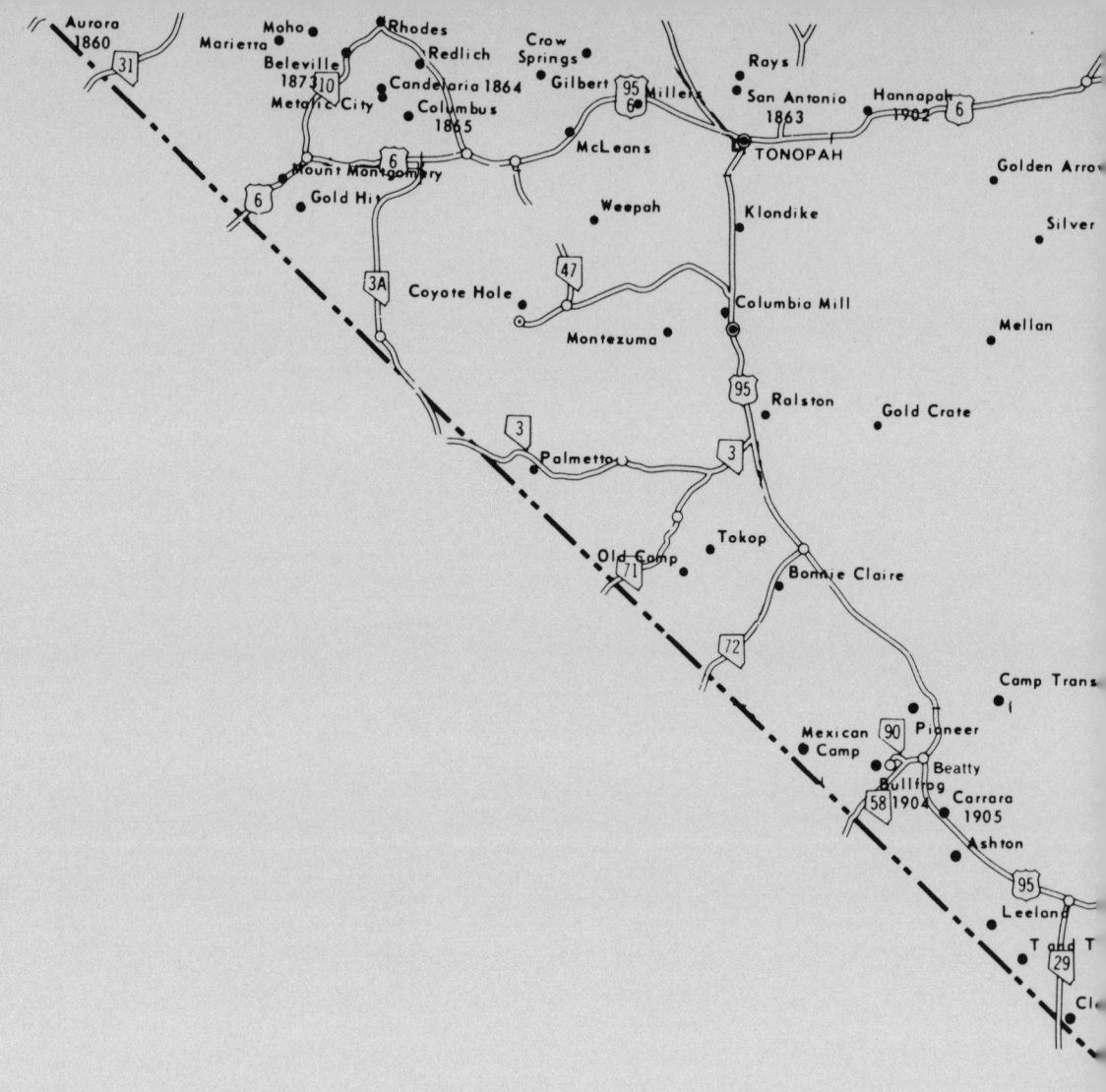